LEARN LAUGH LEAD

HOW TO AVOID A HUGE LEADERSHIT

LEARN LAUGH LEAD

HOW TO AVOID A HUGE LEADERSHIT

BRIAN M HARMAN, MBA, SPSM, LBBP
PHD STUDENT, GLOBAL LEADERSHIP & CHANGE
PEPPERDINE UNIVERSITY

STEPHANIE M TAGLIANETTI, MFA
CALIFORNIA INSTITUTE OF THE ARTS

BUSINESS MANAGEMENT HALLMARK
SAN FRANCISCO, CALIFORNIA

To Scott, our Publicist.
This book is dedicated to you and inspired by your likeness. We cherish your friendship, laughter, love and leadership. Thank you, truly, for leading by example.

Special thanks to Kelsey, Cliff, Cristina, and Michael

TABLE OF CONTENTS

FOREWORD

Every leader is one *leadershit* away from a career-killing moment. It's necessary to know how to spot one before it sneaks up on you.

Learn Laugh Lead: How to Avoid a Huge Leadershit is a hilariously entertaining book that provides the equation for telling your personal story and delivering extraordinary leadership in modern times. It's a page-turner filled with golden nuggets of life lessons.

Brian and Stephanie are first-rate storytellers, with a nontraditional book, as you can see from the front cover. They provide a fresh approach to business with examples of why storytelling with humor should be taken seriously for people who want to connect with colleagues and accomplish meaningful things.

As a young college president, I know there's a new wave of leaders out there who can hugely benefit from this book. It's a must-read with a multitude of approaches for inclusion in your professional tool belt.

I'm someone who has dedicated my life to the study of leadership and believe that these two will play a role in cultivating the next generation of leaders. It's a unique blend of wisdom and wit, perfect for business students and aspiring professionals alike.

Enjoy!

Jeff DeFranco, President
Lake Tahoe Community College

PREFACE

A Shart Start

There's been a lot of talk about global warming and its role in catastrophic weather. But the fate of today's corporate climate is even more grim. Temperatures continue to climb, resulting in an international disaster: a category five shitstorm. There will be casualties. Please, make it stop.

This book is an optimism smoothie, relieving the worst (corporate) diarrhea since the pandemic plague of the Middle Ages. Together, we will embark on a visceral journey through the past, present, and future. But first, we must start with your proverbial dirty laundry. I want to show you the difference between *leadership* and *leadershit*. So grab a load of undies, because it's time to clean up and focus on storytelling, humor, and leading the future.

Frustration is always a function of your expectation. Your state of mind creates your thoughts, which create your expectations, which create your attitude, which builds your level of success. In Tarantino-esque form, we're in the middle of Hurricane Shitrina, so let's jump back to the start of the problem.

Optimism is everything. It is the root of self-control and building a positive self-concept. If you solely believe in fate and destiny, you won't realize the importance of self-control in this equation. Things do not just happen to you. If you believe in happenstance, I encourage you to stop reading now and watch Wheel of Fortune... or stuff a quarter in a Zoltar (that robotic fortune teller machine that turns Tom Hanks into a man-child in *Big*. The authors of this book are Xennial/Millennial, born in the 80's and 90's, so expect a lot of totally rad references, dude).

We've all been left with a stain of discomfort, causing feelings of being trapped, general distress and an unreasonable amount of embarrassment. I'm talking about a skid-mark, which is quite unpleasant, but not foreign to any of us (don't lie). TMI?

Think about that feeling now, but not as literally. Imagine a horrible boss, a terrible manager, a foul politician: an overseer who instead of displaying leadership, broadcasts leadershit.

Leadershit skid-marks are the feelings we are left with after a "shitty" experience with someone who could have been a significant influence on us. They made the bed, laid on the bed and shit in the bed. Then they invited us in there with them.

Rather than using their position of influence, they displayed positional power in the form of a skid-mark. Do you remember someone like this? This could be a single memorable experience or a series of them in your career.

Most of us have had good bosses and bad ones. Which are you? Which do you want to be? Do you want to lead a caravan down the Hershey Highway, or be the leading equivalent of Preparation H, providing relief for those who have been experiencing a great deal of pain and discomfort?

Consider me your gastrointestinal therapist, and this is a leadershit intervention!

DoMo Bro

FOMO so I DoMo, Bro? That's slang for "fear of missing out" so I "do more." I dropped out of college four times before finally going back for real. Finding exciting subjects was not a breeze, and I couldn't understand why reading was such a chore for me. In community college (the last time, when I actually finished and transferred to university), I remember having a hard time reading entire chapters. A couple of pages in and my eyes would wander off. 10-12 pages later, I'd be squinting. After another semester, I decided to have my eyes checked.

The optometrist prescribed me with some computer screen-friendly anti-reflective eyeglasses. This didn't fix the problem. I was suckered into buying expensive Ralph Lauren frames like a chump, so if anything I was worse off. But there was no issue with my eyes. My eyes were fine. The stuff I was reading was not okay. Textbooks suck. From Intro to Geography and English 101 in community college, to Advanced Leadership Theory and Qualitative Research Analysis in postgraduate school, textbooks and readings have been a *little* stale. I've asked around - it turns out that books are boring students to death (yes, death! Just trying to save lives here, people!).

This is a leadership development textbook for professionals and students that want to laugh and cry and enjoy a new take on personal development. The books in this field are typically pseudo-research-oriented and jargony loads of poo that people who want to appear intellectual might read. This ain't that. Notice how I used the word "ain't" to prove a point about being too intellectual. I'm really driving a point here.

I remember in my MBA classes, the content was sometimes difficult to translate into everyday life. *How to Avoid a Huge Leadershit* will show you how to be a better leader every day. That, I promise.

You will start by learning from the past - like history, but riddled with stories, metaphors, 90s references and way too many puns. Then, you will focus on *right now* and how to change your state of mind. You will end with learning how to lead the future from our favorite, future-proof leaders.

Y'all ready for this? (I *know* anyone who went to school in the 90's owned *Jock Jams Vol. 1* and this song was probably fundamental to your gym class warm up. Thanks, 2 Unlimited! If you weren't ready for this, you damn well better be!)

INTRODUCTION

This book has three main sections. Here's what you can expect from each: (1) Learn from the Past with storytelling for leaders, (2) Laugh in the Now by changing your state of mind, (3) Lead the Future like a world-class leader.

Learn from the Past:
Modern Day Minstrels

Each year on my mom's birthday, I ask if she wants to go to Medieval Times for dinner so she can remember what life was like when she was a kid. No internet. Access to all of three TV channels. Essentially, the Medieval Period. No?

In medieval times (the time period, not the dinner tournament), kids only had access to technology that originated in a blacksmith's forge. So, I guess my mom's set of jacks and dominoes catapulted her out of the Middle Ages, after all.

Storytelling was a crucial part of the culture back then. Ears were supremely valuable, which is why knights' helmets covered the ears so well. Listening to stories was regarded as an act of love, respect, and honor. And a knight without ears is a leader without a torch. Storytelling is the language of leaders, but leaders must focus *first* on listening (with those super essential ears).

Leaders must be students to learn from the past and every moment in between. Listening is also an excellent way to learn and prepare the stories you tell at your moments of influence. That's the difference between leading and advising. I can tell you not to be cheap. That's easy. But instead, if I tell you a story that shows you exactly what it means to be cheap and why that quality has an adverse effect, it will be memorable and lasting - all while I convey my point with humor. (I will tell this story in a few pages).

I recently took a survey ranking the skills that a great leader needs. Listening is rated among the essential skills, but also among the least practiced skill. Surprised?

How do you improve your listening skills? Act as a student. Learn to lead like you're a student. It means that sometimes you need to shut the f-ck up. It's simple. Practice being quiet. Go to a Zen center. Take a vow of silence. Become a monk for a day. Try to think of the last time you were quiet. Repeat. Cool. Now continue listening.

After reading this book, you will be able to generate influence through stories. Storytelling, like great leadership, is timeless. I want you to picture a toolkit right now. It's got different compartments, and you can pull what you need from it at different times. There's a "fundamentals" compartment: listening, reading, speaking and writing are already in there. But you need to practice using them. These skills are like power tools. You can't just pick one up and swing it around like you know how to use it. You have to start practicing with small projects, first.

There's another compartment that is just as important: creativity. You'll need these tools to develop your storytelling skills. You'll use creativity to relate to your audience. You'll need to be able to adapt to different methods of style and delivery. Preparation is required to meet the audience's needs with structured content. We will arm you with a story arsenal to get you started.

The final compartment: attitude. Your state of mind. It's going to be different for each audience, and you need to know how and when those changes need to happen.

Change the Now: Affirming Awesome

Why didn't my mom just sell our house and invest in Apple back on their IPO day in 1980? Because nobody can see the future. In global commerce, there are always invisible opportunities left behind in time. But these chances are in abundance.

I want to be a writer; here I am writing. Opportunities are everywhere, see? Leaders must adapt their state of mind and take control of their lives. What can you control? Everything. Do you complain? Why? You can manage that, so don't. Control your opportunities the same way. Find them.

Our thoughts generate our universe. I lead as a result of my self-control and optimism. Every morning, I write down my goals, in detail most days. I write why I have these goals (reasons) and why I need to accomplish them (more reasons). These are short-term and long-term goals, and they're continually changing and gaining more significance to me. So I remind myself of them every day, every morning.

You can live in the present moment by setting and achieving goals. The more you do this, the more success you'll have. If you are feeling fresh and inspired, add some written affirmations to boot. They can be utterly mundane.

Something like: *I am awesome, I am awesome, I am awesome.* Goals that aren't written down are collections of dust bunnies floating around on the floor of your subconscious. No purpose. No chance of becoming anything, well, other than a dust bunny in your brain. You have to set goals, write them down for the future, and lead now. That's living in the present. Now, for the future.

Lead the Future:
Unwasted Potential

Learn from the best to become the best. In this section of the book, you'll hear stories from our favorite leaders. But it's not all pretty because even the best leaders aren't perfect. They have failed. A LOT. They got dirty, and they had some proverbial laundry of their own to clean.

How hard you try at achieving your goals is equal to how much you truly believe in yourself. Said alternatively, discipline equals pride. I believe in myself, so I try hard to achieve my goals. I don't make excuses or tell people about things I'll never do. Are you an "idea person" that's not accomplishing anything? How's that working for ya? I thought so. Know it all? How's that working for ya? Please keep reading. I want to help you. That's on my goal list (see what I did there? Helping others through my writing is a goal. Are you picking up what I'm putting down? Well, I mean you're literally picking up what I put down if you're reading this book).

Why do we study leaders? Because in physics, *potential* means wasted energy. I don't want to be a contracted spring all tightened up like a useless ball of metal. I, like you, want to become more successful and unlock my potential as a leader. The leaders we interviewed are folks who value trust, authenticity, and self-control. They are people who tell good stories and put everything on the line to achieve their vision. Some of them arrived at their careers off the beaten path, and hearing their stories will show you how to be a leadershit-free leader.

In this book, you will learn how to maximize your affective communication and conscious mind, and improve your cognitive skills that impact leadership development. That's fancy talk for becoming happy and prosperous. Let go of competition within yourself and with others. Make a positive impact on those around you. Our storytelling and communication techniques will help you better relate to people. You will learn how to live in the moment, happily and successfully. But we've got some work to do. So, let's begin.

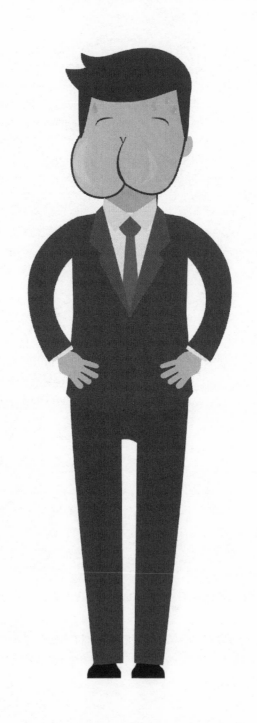

Mr. Butts, Sales Manager
P & O Outsourcing Partners

A loud clock hangs on an office wall. It slowly ticks as a tall, staunch businessman, Mr. Butts, stands at a podium, in front of the sales team. A mirror hangs against the back wall of the conference room, and he notices a few hairs out of place. He brushes them down with his fingers.

A decisive black suit, imperfectly tailored, shows that he put forth just enough effort. Not too much, but a mediocre amount. He taps a small stack of index cards softly against the podium, too close to the microphone, in sync with the clock. He looks down at the cards and speaks the words he scribbled down on them the night before. "So, I just want to start off by saying I might stumble through this a little bit. As you all know, I'm really not that organized and wrote down some stuff late last night that I can hardly even read, so just bear with me here."

The sales team slouches in their chairs, anticipating a long-winded meeting. With each word Mr. Butts speaks, a horrible smell grows around him. With each phrase, the scent grows into an object. A physical representation of his words before the team. And as he speaks, the object's shape is more recognizable, and the smell becomes more familiar.

His words grow into an enormous pile of shit. A failure, literally represented in the shit-pile. But where did he go wrong?

LEARN FROM THE PAST

Storytelling for Leaders

Why Tell Stories:
Billy Joel and the Basics

It's always been a matter of trust. Cue: Billy Joel's 1986 hit "A Matter of Trust." What was this fluffy-haired white guy from Long Island singing about? Trust, duh. We posed a simple question to several business entrepreneurs: "What's the most important quality a leader must have?" Above strategic planning, social influence, listening, and feedback, trusted relationships ranked first. Even Billy Joel knows what's up when it comes to leadership. Respect, Billy.

Today's corporate professionals and business owners alike voted that trust is key to success. Networking can be fun and notoriously opportunistic and advantageous, but it's the close-knit, inner-circle type relationships that will really thrust your career. Thrust with trust!

Sure, it's easy to say, "build trust," but countless movies and songs tell us how hard it is to build trust ... essentially saying "trust no one." A famous quote from Scarface comes to mind: "watch who you trust - even your teeth bite your tongue now and then." Damn. So, how do you build trusted relationships, especially in a corporate setting?

You have to become a trusted leader. Leaders establish trust through credibility, care, communication, and giving. Their stories are the way they communicate these behaviors. And you may have heard - storytelling is the language of leaders. Too many leaders communicate lessons with brief statements like, "Never stop improving" or "be decisive." That's not how you create an emotional connection to inspire people. Great leaders tell stories to create meaningful interactions and learning opportunities. I'm not talking about the long, drawn out sort of stories you hear from strangers at the train station, either. I'm talking about those quick stories that you remember and retell later on.

Mastery of impactful storytelling has other benefits. It allows you to deliver content memorably and deliberately. It improves your ability to improvise and relate to people. It is the tool that ignites connections among our species and the way tradition translates into honor.

Generating influence through storytelling is a fundamental behavior for leaders to exhibit their purpose and vision. Put some good ol' stories in your arsenal for daily use. But more importantly, be able to tell a good story.

What a Story Does
If They Don't Suck, They Stick

Thanks for hanging, but we had a feeling you would. Why? Because everyone loves a good story. And the very best stories are the ones you can re-tell the same exact way each time because they are awesome. I promised you a story about being cheap, didn't I? Here it goes.

When I was a kid, my grandfather told me a story about a man in England, who lived before the London Bridge was built. A guy named John Overs. He created his wealth by transporting people by ferry from one side of the Thames River to the other. Mr. Overs was a well-known cheapskate, and he regularly found ways to save money. In a bastardly attempt to keep the money he had to shell out for feeding his servants each day, John cooked up a plan to fake his death; he thought the servants would fast for the day in his honor. But, when someone Scrooge-like dies, people aren't all that sad. And John was shocked to learn that his servants weren't fasting as a courtesy to their dearly departed as he'd planned. Upon finding John Overs wrapped up in a burial shroud, his servants celebrated. They danced around his body, drank all of his wine and, ironically, ate all of his food. When he couldn't bare playing dead any longer, in true curmudgeon form, John tried to spoil their fun. He unwrapped himself from the burial shroud and rose up, playing the role of chastising ghost (damn, there's a lot of semblance to *A Christmas Carol*). All Ghost-John did was frighten everyone; so much that one servant grabbed an oar and beat the crap out of John until he was indeed dead. Ultimately, John Overs was killed for being a spiteful cheapass.

My grandfather was a leadership role model, and there's a reason I've clung to the way he told me this story for the first time and each time after. When I was four or five years old, I just thought the story about John Overs was funny, and I couldn't capture the big picture. 30 years later, I still remember cheapass J.O. and realize why my grandfather told me that story each time I find myself trying to save a buck for the sake of being cheap. He knew the impact a good story could have, and he often taught me life's most valuable lessons in the form of a story. More about him later.

Fact:
Business is Personal

People aren't compelled by facts alone. They don't make decisions based on facts. Emotion is the only way to make meaningful connections because people base their decisions on emotions. Storytelling is a way to elicit an emotional response to help people make a decision or support your vision. Thus, emotions drive decisions.

Pretend your brain is a car. Your emotional brain is the powerful engine, and your rational brain is the chassis, providing a frame of support.

Stories are extended metaphors, and associative thinking is one of the best ways to help your listeners connect the dots. Always think about how you will build out the comparison in your story with metaphors or analogies. Sir Paul Smith says that if you can't find a metaphor, just ask someone. If you need a metaphor for parking at a busy market, ask people what they don't like about it. My wife says, "I don't like when people bump into me; I need my space. And an empty spot in the Trader Joe's parking lot looks like a swarm of flies on shit." There's your metaphor: a swarm of flies!

Starting at the end can make it easier. Failure can sometimes breed failure. How can you turn a team loss into a win instead of another miss? Find a metaphor. If your team likes basketball, you could tell the story of Michael Jordan, who invariably maintains that his failures are the only reason for his success. Buy a Michael Jordan poster for the office wall if you have to. Keep it real. Concrete stories that are specific to your work culture and the people in your environment make the best stories. Get too abstract, and your ideas will float away. The civil rights activist, Dr. Martin Luther King Jr., made sure his views never came off like a mission statement. His words were spoken as dreams and visions for a better future. And he kept it real.

It Was a Dark Night
(Version 1)

Know someone who tells stories that are utterly pointless? I sure as hell do! I've been to countless meetings where the team leader veers off, transporting everyone to a far-off planet with a meaningless story that is entirely irrelevant to what we're (supposed to be) talking about. Only to be followed up with, "but I digress." Yeah, you did!

Stories teach us lessons or reveal something to the listener in a relatable and memorable way. But you need to know how to tell a story the right way, to make this effective. Sometimes learning from mistakes is the best way to move forward. So, let's start off with a bad story:

'Twas an extremely dark and mysterious night as I stoodeth on mine stout two fortitudinous feet alongside a tall stone castle mure. Mine armor wast as dark as a swamp, as plaited as a feast, and as ornate as a queen. The whey-face moon gleamed as mine charming knight's smile glareth through mine helmet's visor. I exude a quiet magnificence from mine bold ancestors.

This armor is secure, all fortnight long
Mine ears art safe, though mine bottom shall chafe
Don't maketh me chuckle; I'll blow out mine buckle -
Fie! Too late! A shart wast mine fate!

Point of the story? Epic fail. There was no point, which is why this was a *shitty* story. There was no appeal to analyze (aside from the vagrant use of the English language with a shart as the payoff). We will review proper storytelling techniques and examples of persuasive storytelling in this section so you can use storytelling to increase your influence.

Let's try again...

It Was a Dark Night, Again
(Version 2)

In the midst of the Crusades, a knight built a name for himself. Not on honor, but vanity. Sir Cassius was as commanding as he was arrogant. He was known well in England as a narcissist who took the maidenheads of many women, adorning himself with a trophy of his accomplishments: a locket that held a strand of hair from each woman he deflowered. In fact, he never overcame a single thing without bestowing some token of victory upon himself as a reminder.

Sir Cassius led a cavalry through many victories against the Muslims. Near the end of The Fourth Crusade, he led a particularly victorious battle, where the Muslim infantry was wholly conquered by Sir Cassius and his knights. Before leading his men home, Sir Cassius required his men to raid the Muslim camp. "Take as much loot as you may carry on your back and steed. But the finest will be worn upon my back." Sir Cassius adorned himself with the most magnificent armory of the Muslim infantry and carried two large sacks of their gold-plated goblets, lanterns, and jewels. He led his knights homeward, their loot clamoring in a boisterous hum with each gallop of their steeds.

At nightfall, Sir Cassius told the men not to light their torches. He knew how to navigate home in the blackest night, according to the stars alignment. Again, his vanity reigned at highest rank as they rode on

When they approached the castle, the king's men were alarmed to hear the terrible clashing of men approaching in the dark without torches. Thought to be invaded by enemies of the Crusades, the castle guards lined the fortress with crossbows and firearms pointed straight at the dark knights approaching. A castle guard called out from the walls, "Continue on and you will be met with a quick death," but Sir Cassius could not hear beyond the galloping of horses, the clashing of the loot and his own blustering. Again, the castle guard yelled out, but this time "Fire!" Still, Sir Cassius and his men gloated and could not hear the warning. And so they were fired upon. Two rounds of the guards' armory took each knight off his horse, and the horses fled with much of the loot, in panic.

For a knight without ears is a leader without a torch.

How?
Setting it Up

The best stories are humble, easy to understand and remember, infectious, inspirational, and universal. Leaders can use stories to motivate others and convey an impactful message, but there are foundations of storytelling that you must establish. Let's use the previous story about Sir Cassius as an example of how to set up a story.

Setting

The setting is not the most important story element to convey your message, but the Middle Ages was chosen for a reason. I set my story in the Middle Ages because when a listener hears the word "knight," they already have a visceral image of what that looks like. I don't have to paint a picture for them because there's already a foundation. You know folks who tell stories and "lay the backstory on thick?" I totally avoided all of that by selecting a time and place that most readers will already have an understanding of. This is especially important when you think about who you are telling your stories to. Always think of the team, the environment, and your shared knowledge. Make your stories relatable in some way.

Character

The most critical element is the character. In a story, you traditionally have a protagonist. Don't confuse this word with "hero." It simply refers to the main character of your story. This is the character you are going use to convey your point. They don't have to be "good," per se. Think about Sir Cassius. He's the protagonist, but he's also kind of an a-hole, right?

Plot

Your character should have some sort of conflict if you're going to teach a lesson to your listener. And as leaders, that's what we want to do, no? Use a story to convey a point. And this is where the plot comes in. The plot of the story is *how* you communicate your point. The plot is merely the action. It expresses what our character wants in a series of events. And establishing the motivation of your character and some sort of conflict is how you will teach your listener.

So, what did our character want? A good leader has a worthy objective and clear mission. In the case of Sir Cassius, he wanted to be well-known. But the root of this desire was narcissism and vanity. And what was in his way of getting it? Sir Cassius sought power. And he had that. But he became a glutton for it, and ultimately that was his conflict. So, he was in his own way of succeeding. Not because he couldn't attain power, but because he wanted too much of it. He's a leader who doesn't share the spotlight and uses fear to motivate others, and trust is the foundation of good working relationships.

Good leadership always begins with yourself, but it cannot stop there. Having a mission, values, and objective is important, and Sir Cassius was "all about the numbers" with no regard for the "big picture." Classic shitty leader, right? He's in it for his own advancement - just trying to gain power and fame without consideration for anyone else. And he ultimately gets himself, and all of his followers killed.

Build and Tell Your Personal Story

About Brian (Bad Version)

I, Brian M. Harman, MBA, am an American businessman that has been working in corporate leadership and supply chain management since 2005. I've studied global finance, administration, and management sciences at Oxford and Pepperdine, earning an MBA degree from Pepperdine University, where I am currently completing my Ph.D. dissertation in Global Leadership and Change. My specialized work in negotiation and management has driven my career in construction, biotechnology, and pharmaceutical manufacturing. Outside of my corporate job, I focus on leadership psychology, research, consulting, teaching, and writing. I hold certifications as a Senior Professional in Supply Management (SPSM) as well as Lean Six Sigma Black Belt (LBBP) for continuous improvement methodologies. I have been recognized twice by the Council for Supply Chain Management Professionals (CSCMP) and have been awarded academic grants for graduate research. I reside in the San Francisco Bay Area, California, USA.

LAME@$%^&*

That was the lamest story ever. I'd be shocked if you even read all that. It was not good. In fact, it was not a story. It was more like a set of resume notes that said nothing about a real human being. But how many times have we come across introductions like that, or even introduced ourselves in a similar way to others? Pretty damn often, no?

To master the art of personal and business storytelling, you must evolve your key messages into explicit stories that transform audiences and initiate action through a personal and emotional connection. They can take time to develop. Presentations that flourish and cause meaningful change all have something in common: they use the timeless principles of narrative to engage people and rally support. There was no narrative in that first version, just facts and resume pieces, one after the next. And I'm sorry I had to put you through that.

After researching the most effective speakers and speeches of all time, I will now teach you how to consistently deliver unparalleled messages. You will put principles into action when you write your own story, then become unstoppable!

About Brian (Better Version)

I am first a loving husband, and also a father, brother, musician, dog-lover, and vegetarian (apart from consuming the occasional oyster and Peruvian ceviche). I was fortunate to marry my first childhood love, who is now the mother of my beautiful son. She inspires me to thrive as a global leader, writer, educator, and scholar.

But things aren't always what they seem. There were several critical turning points in my life that changed my path. These were times when I wanted to give up. But these significant events took me from the road of a young, dumb, college dropout and troublemaker with no future, to that of a strategic supply chain professional who works for a leading biotechnology company.

My favorite life-changing moment was when I married my wife. I wanted to provide her with a better future, so I went back to school shortly after our engagement began. But it wasn't a breeze. There were unforeseen circumstances that made it much harder to walk down this new path I paved.

I was diagnosed with a rare disease called Fibrous Dysplasia. Four surgeries, 14 metal screws and four metal rods later, I walk a bit stiffer and have limited neck mobility. It took much adjusting, as you can imagine. Cue the robot jokes. This was a challenging time. And each break I had from class terms, it seemed I was back in the hospital for surgery again.

One of the reasons I work in biotech now is because I know what it's like to suffer from a rare disease. So currently I work with a company that develops genetic therapies and cures for rare diseases, saving the lives of thousands of children.

Now, I want to share some of my secrets. First: my secret to life is laughter. After my first spine surgery, I was a miserable jerk. Friends and family only helped me out of pity, but I did not deserve their help or care. The second time around, I decided I would use that traumatic event to force change into my life. I chose to laugh it off. After all, growing up with three brothers means I was always laughing (or fighting) during childhood, so I knew I had a sense of humor in there somewhere, matched with a competitive brother "I can do anything" mentality.

Second secret: Peru and USA are my favorite countries in the world. My favorite food is a Peruvian dish called "Tortilla del Abuela," and my wife was born in Lima, Peru, where I am teaching global leadership to MBA students from South America. If food is how people gather and connect, Peru is winning.

When young leaders ask me for tips, I always tell them my secrets: laughter, meditation, exercise, and written goals. These are the daily activities that help me reach my 1-year, 5-year, and 20-year goals. Oh ya, and a dirty bedroom is a dirty life. It's true. Remember that. You can tell a lot about a person by their bedroom. Clean up.

My last secret: I sincerely want to help others find happiness. Yes, it was shocking to find out I was going to have a tough life after my diagnosis. But the proudest day of my life was marrying my wife, and she deserves a husband who will never give up on happiness. I remember that I couldn't stop smiling on my wedding day because the only thing I ever wanted in life since the age of 12 was to be married to her. Yes, I cried. People around you vibe off of your vibes, and I want to have positive vibes, even if that means shedding a few happy tears.

My life has adventure, love, and laughter. Besides traveling, I enjoy sailing in the San Francisco Bay. At times, when things seem terrible, I just remember how lucky I am to have survived a rare disease that kills people. Things aren't always peachy. I struggle and have challenges, daily. I don't believe my life is better or worse than anyone else's. I think that people are exciting and intriguing, and we should strive to help each other through life's struggles.

How to Create your Personal Story

This story above is a small window into my life. Hopefully, you can see me as a person now, not just a resume. My story is mine, so I tell it proudly. How will you tell yours? Take your time, don't worry about it being perfect, and most importantly, tell it! People want to know you. We live in a transactional task-task-task society, so you must determine your purpose to avoid getting lost in the business of a busy life. Having a personal story and mission are great ways to check in with your "big picture" and set goals.

First things first. Write down answers to all the following questions:

1. What do you want people to say about you when you die?
2. What are three things you can't live without?

3. You get news that you're dying in three months from a terminal disease: how do you spend that time before you pass?
4. What are you most proud of?
5. What are your favorite things to do?
6. Who are your favorite people?
7. If you could do anything, what would you do?

The answers to these questions will help you form your vision statement (an elevator pitch of *you*). That will be 2-3 sentences that mark the beginning of your story. Then, you back up your vision statement by stating the reasons why. Think about the same list of questions above, and answer "why?" for each one. Begin with childhood and family, then relive your turning points and challenges, with a conclusion that brings it all together. Don't be afraid to become the underdog in your story as I did with my health diagnosis.

The personal story should always be a draft. In other words, it shouldn't be perfect. I did not make a bunch of edits to my account. I told it from the heart and made it human. I know with certainty that you probably didn't connect with all of it, but maybe one or two parts, perhaps. That's all you can ask for from people, and that's all you can hope to give to people. A few reliable connections and a smile. Telling our personal stories and bringing up hardships can be difficult. Be open and vulnerable to explore and share with people. I'm sure I will re-read my story and create a new draft according to where I'm at now, but I will try not to go crazy fixing it because it shouldn't be a written masterpiece. Your personal story is just an informal conversation about yourself. My "aha" moment was when I decided the second surgery wasn't going to be an excuse for being a jerk any longer. I hope you can learn from my past mistake there.

Build Up Your Story Arsenal

Feel free to use these stories, that's what they're here for! Construct a bunch of your own though, too. This will take time, but a story in your personal narrative is much more emotionally vested for both you and your listener. A good story is authentic and relatable. So don't tell stories that don't relate to you, and especially don't tell stories that don't apply to you. Anytime you are in a position of influence, being interviewed, having a meaningful conversation, etcetera, try to use stories to convey key messaging instead of short, shitty answers. They're much more powerful and memorable. Below you can read a few of my stories.

Cultura Malentendido:
Saying the Wrong Thing and Making it Right

I recently went on a surfing trip with several colleagues. As a rookie, I was excited to thrash the mellow waves of the Pacific Coast, south of the California border. I was gonna shred some serious gnar and hang ten on the curl of a killer wave. And I did, bro.

After carving a day full of wavy glory, the gang had quite an appetite swelling. It was time to hit up a local taco stand. Just outside the beautiful little community of Las Gaviotas, we found our dude. The local chef welcomed us with open arms and a high five. But then, I encountered an unfortunate miscommunication. One that I won't soon forget.

Since we were in Mexico, I decided to show off and speak in the native tongue. My rusty Spanish rarely makes a guest appearance, so I figured I'd start by ordering a beer. "Hola, amigo! Puedo tener una cerveza, por favor!" The conversation continues. He asks how I like Mexico so far and I reply, "me encanto mucho tu pais." Thinking that I just gave the ultimate compliment, telling my beloved new taco amigo that "I love his country very much," I was confused when his smile curled and furrowed into a confused pucker. Something I said? He says back to me, "so you pooped a lot since you been here, eh amigo?" Apparently, my "encanto" came out sounding like "cago," the Spanish word for pooping. He then said, "well, gringo, you are gonna be pooping a lot after this spicy not-for-gringo taco especial." He shakes some extra hot sauce on top of my plate. We all had a good laugh and raised our glasses.

Laughing is the universal way to wipe the slate clean after miscommunications. Laughing will always help you start over. Also, just a tip, don't tell people you came to shit in their country.

Honor, Homage, and the Piano Man

Before the notable Theatre Arts Program (TAP) existed at Sacred Heart University (SHU), there was a small club of theatre players who were dedicated to making their little club a full-blown program. The "SHU Players." And among the most dedicated of the Players was a guy named Chris Bowley. He was considered the physical embodiment of the spirit and goals of the organization at large.

Chris Bowley passed away from complications with pneumonia, and the SHU Players wanted to commemorate his exceptional dedication to their club. Each year, a student who exhibits his same commitment and enthusiasm is awarded the Chris Bowley Award. But the tradition in his honor doesn't stop there.

Chris's favorite song was "Piano Man" (bringing it back to Billy Joel, here). And before the opening show of each performance, TAP members join hands on stage and sing "Piano Man." There is a sense of love and community, and this tradition still carries on today. Chris knew that the small club could turn into something much grander. His spirit and legacy live on because he was committed to seeing the big picture.

Jerry Goehring and the Red Herring

What's next? The Theatre Arts Program at SHU became fully developed in 2009. The Director, Jerry Goehring, wanted to make a lasting impression on the school with the program's inaugural musical performance.

He didn't want to put on a classic show. Instead, he wanted to take a stance - he wanted to show that the program was going to be fresh, forward-thinking and contemporary. And that the school was ready for it.

So, what show did Jerry do? He selected a controversial musical: *Rent*. This was a huge risk at a private, Catholic university. The content of the show is centered around sex and drugs and rock-and-roll... death... gay culture. But he knew that you have to take risks. You have to make people uncomfortable. And you have to take an active stance, and back it up. Did Jerry have push-back for the debut show? Sure! He countered any arguments about the surface content in the show. He knew that those cases avoided the central issue: that the show was something different. Something new. Not for the world, but for the school community, especially in a performance setting. And the themes were important and entirely relevant for the students. Jerry pushed the boundaries, and the show was a hit on campus. The on-campus priest even reflected on the content in a sermon following opening night.

Jerry knew that the show was groundbreaking and that it would set the precedence for shows to follow. And it did. Jerry went on to direct *Little Shop of Horrors* (a show in which a man-eating plant takes over skid row, and ultimately the world), *Spring Awakening* (sex, suicide, abortions) and *Nunsense* (a show that premiered in drag - men dressed as nuns). All at a Catholic school.

Jerry had a vision that honored Chris Bowley's dedication. Luckily, he had resources to help him when people pushed back. Before rehearsals began for *Spring Awakening*, Jerry brought in expert coaches, like Duncan Sheik (the Tony award-winning composer for *Spring Awakening* who is also known for his hit single "Barely Breathing"). Along with Duncan, members of the original Broadway cast coached the student performers with the roles they debuted on Broadway. The musical director at SHU, Leo Carusone, was a musical director/conductor for numerous shows on Broadway, and he wrote all of the vocal and musical arrangements for the *Nunsense* musical series. Jerry ran practicums lead by experts in their field, continuing to develop the program at Sacred Heart University. And now the theatre presence at SHU has evolved from a club into a real program, and ultimately into a program that offers a major. High resources, high risk.

We're always told to "know our audience." But sometimes you have to know yourself and what's important to you. If you have a strong stance, people will listen. For Jerry, it was all well-received. He went on to produce a Tony and Grammy-nominated show on Broadway and still directs the program at Sacred Heart University. Chris would be proud.

The Glory of the Story

In summary, let's acknowledge the history and importance of storytelling. It's the best way to inspire, teach and connect with your team, so you leave them thinking about your message long after your moment of influence. Some of the most celebrated leaders also happen to be regarded as exceptional communicators and compelling storytellers. We should seek to tell lasting stories, instead of just talking up shit in a moment of potential influence. Be unforgettable, set your story up right, build up your story arsenal and relate to others with personal and emotional experiences. But remember, "b-tch, be humble (Kendrick Lamar)."

Mr. Butts, Sales Manager
P & O Outsourcing Partners

Mr. Butts tries to figure out where he went wrong last time. He thinks back to the night before his meeting, rushing through his note cards without much careful thought. The next day, he wasn't prepared. He hadn't connected with his team, so he didn't know how to speak to them. In fact, he realizes that he doesn't even know the names of everyone on his team.

Becoming more self-aware, the lingering smell from his last meeting starts to dissipate.

A mysterious, dark figure rises from the corner of the conference room and approaches Mr. Butts at the podium. The shady character is drawn to the fluorescent overhead light reflecting in the mirror, like a moth. The disfigured image starts to look more familiar until Mr. Butts realizes he is staring at himself. He is the villain. He is the one limiting his chance at successful leadership.

LAUGH IN THE NOW

Change Your State of Mind

Laughter is Faster

An infectious laugh truly is infectious. Laughter is the emotional contagion that is most easily spread, curing a stale office environment and bringing joy - to the people! By the people! For the people! Laughter is a f-cking democracy! In fact, Abe Lincoln himself was a great storyteller and often prefaced important discussions with humorous stories. When his cabinet members didn't find a particular story funny, Lincoln said, "Gentlemen, why don't you laugh? With the fearful strain that is upon me night and day, if I did not laugh I should die, and you need this medicine as much as I do." Abe Lincoln: great leader, loves to laugh. He knew the importance of laughter and humor. The best leaders I know also happen to be the funniest and wittiest. Having fun is better than not having fun, am I right?

Take the initiative to make your work environment more fun. My friend Chris invented a game called "*Bueller*-ing." I'm not sure how it happened, or why. But it's a simple game. All you need to do is rhyme a word with Ferris "Bueller" in a sentence, question, or (the best way) as an insult. I love teaching it to folks at work and seeing the creative ways they "Bueller." For example:

Stephanie: Should we grab a Ferris *Brew*-ler after work on Friday?
Brian: Yes, definitely. I like Stella Artois cuz I'm Ferris *Cool*-er.
Stephanie: Or cuz you're a Ferris *Tool*-er.
Brian: No... I'm Ferris Rad-ular?
Stephanie (facepalm): Brian, that one doesn't work. The word has to rhyme without being forced. Go back to Ferris *School*-er, you Ferris *Looo*-ser.

Work with people that make you laugh, or at least be the fun one on your team if nobody else is. That is something you do have control over.

How Are You Funny?

Being vulnerable and honest leads to the best form of humor. People love to laugh at things that they can relate to or have experienced in some way themselves. Think about stand-up comedians who draw from their own experiences and tell jokes about uncomfortable situations we can all relate to. Because we've experienced them ourselves. Sebastian Maniscalco (famously known for jokes that leave him saying "aren't you embarrassed?") succeeds at this in his stand-up, often ruminating on the everyday interactions we have with people. He says, "if I can relate to the joke, it's going to be funny." Honesty in humor will help instill trust.

When someone asks me how to use humor in storytelling and presentations, I will never tell them about the use of a self-deprecating sense of humor. For example, if I'm nervous before a presentation, I won't say something like, "I'm a little nervous, and I'm sure the folks sitting closest to me will agree that it *is* possible to smell fear." Sure, I'll get a few laughs, but I'm not starting off from a strong and confident place. I'm starting from a position of weakness. If I want to be honest about my nerves, that's relatable. And you shouldn't be afraid to laugh at yourself, either. But a first impression shouldn't be an attack on yourself. You want to stand on a stronger leg than that.

Instead, intelligent wit, relatable stories, and an animated attitude - that'll bring in the laughs. A few examples of things that are universally funny: voices/impersonations (even bad ones, sometimes those are funnier), props, accents (in good humor, not making fun of people), anecdotes, jokes, pictures/comics, surprises, punchlines, dances, games, and stories. Find a way to be honest, above all. Because remember, it's always "A Matter of Trust."

The Psychology Behind Laughing

Laughter is connected to leadership because of its social power. Laughter can wipe the slate clean when things go awry. It can build immediate acceptance in a group setting and establish rapport faster than through talking. It diffuses tension and erases stress.

If you think about the physical responses, what happens when we laugh? Our chin rises, exposing our neck. As a primitive response, exposing your neck means you are providing instant approval, vulnerability, or acceptance. You trust the person enough to laugh with them. When you don't trust someone, their jokes aren't funny for this very reason. Your brain won't let you become vulnerable to them because you don't trust them. Wait a minute; laughter equals trust? Leadership requires humor?

How can you build trust and humor as a leader? Tell funny stories in vulnerable settings (or at least try to). By forcing vulnerability, you are reprogramming your mind to accept and embrace vulnerability (and weakness), instead of rejecting it, which is most people's natural tendency.

Here's one thing we will probably agree on: being a humorous leader that can joke with friends about dropping the kids off at the pool in the office restroom is gross, but better than a bossy ass that uses positional power to dictate orders like a tyrant.

What's In My Control?

"You have a nice smile." Thanks. "Your positive attitude at work is something I really admire about you." Woah. Like Keanu, woaaaah. Complimenting people on things within their self-control is much more personal. And powerful!

The psychology of self-control and achievement is simple. As shown in the example above, it's great to be told that you have a friendly smile, but a compliment about something that's within your range of self-control? Like your dedication? That's an unforgettable way to get someone's attention and admiration. Instead of saying, "you have a great smile," you could say, "it's really awesome that you smile so much. Your attitude makes me happier than I was before we met." Boom. Gonna be smiling for days after a statement like that.

Some things are apparently out of our control. Back to my spine. I have a bone disease that resulted in two neck surgeries, two lower back surgeries and ultimately the fusions of my cervical spine (skull to C5) and lumbar spine (L4-L5). These operations meant I would lose some of the ability to turn my back/neck to see the world around me. And at first, I couldn't see beyond my new limitations.

After the first lower back surgery, I was a victim to the world and a coward to the pain. I was weak. And this "bottomed out" feeling went on for a while. I felt like crap and was a major jerk to everyone around me. I knew I had to make a change, and it would need to start with me and the things that are within my control.

A year later when my next closest disc collapsed (also lower back), I went back in for major surgery. And this time I decided to change my attitude. I used all of my energy and self-control to become a different person. I first had to think about the limitations differently. I realized that I didn't lose the ability to see the world around me, I just had to alter how I move my body to look at things.

It's easy to use a traumatic experience to harness positive energy. It's an excuse to be better. Because I decided to make a change and do something that was important to me, my relationships changed, too. I corrected my diet, lost weight, stopped complaining, had lots of energy, went back to college, got a new job, and the list goes on. My marriage improved. My healing time after surgery was much quicker than the first one. My relationships with my family members became stronger.

A couple of years later when I got the news about a bone disease in my cervical spine (neck), it didn't bother me. No tears were shed. I knew it would be another challenge and an opportunity to become a better man, no matter the obstacle.

You can't just hope for the best. Hope is a waste of time; ambition is what pushes you forward. In Spanish, "hope" and "waiting" are the same word. So don't waste your time waiting and hoping. You can institute change with your ambitious self-control.

Happiness is a State of Mind

My grandpa used to tell me this story about a woman named Petunia whom he met in a legal office back in the 1940s. They interacted a few brief times, and he thought she was stunning. He even used the word "breathtaking." The problem was, he couldn't bring himself to ask her out.

She was tall and lean with light, wavy hair. And she always looked elegant. But she expressed herself strongly. That's what my grandpa liked about her most, and what he was intimidated by most. He said she looked like she walked right out of a poster or magazine advertisement for the latest fashion (move over, Doris Day). They exchanged witty banter several times each month, but he couldn't muster up the courage to ask her out on a date. He was going to move onto new endeavors and wouldn't be coming by her office anymore. But my Poppi always said that when he looked back at this time in his life, he remembered being really good with time. He never wasted it. He had three jobs and slept standing up on many occasions. As a lawyer and doctor, he'd often fall asleep with books in his hand. He said to me, "make good use of your time because time will pass whether you like it or not." And the story ended there.

He told me this story about a year before he died. But how can he say that he never wasted time and continually tell me the story about this Petunia lady? Ya, I was confused too.

Almost ten years later, when I was in high school, I had to do a family research project, and I started asking my mom about my grandparents. She said grandpa met grandma in a legal office early in his career. No way! That woman, Petunia, was my grandma! But my grandma's name wasn't Petunia, so I was confused, again. Apparently, my grandma used that name because she loved flowers and never gave strangers her real name. I still didn't understand. I was baffled. Why didn't he just tell me? He said he didn't want to waste time, so he just asked her out? It seems he knew time would pass no matter what, so why squander his time and miss the opportunity to be with his one true love (you dirty dog, Poppi, you).

There is no substitute for proper time management because it gives you more time for face-to-face business, personal relationships, and new connections. Next time you can't find the confidence to ask a question, just remember that time is going to pass either way.

Powered by Optimism

You are in control of the path of your life. Whether that leads to failure, success, peace and joy or heartache. Complaining, blaming, and making excuses are all results of dangerous thinking. Like your shadow, your thoughts follow you everywhere, and your views frame your character.

Steve Covey said, "frustration is a function of expectation." Change your expectations, and you'll lose that frustration. Positive thinking allows you to generate better expectations. Better aspirations lead you to believe in yourself and practice the discipline needed to meet your goals. Since this all starts with being happy, let's go back to that. Happiness is the root of optimism. And optimism is your source of power (corny, but true).

If you're building a framework for leadership, the base that gets everything else rolling needs to be positive. And to construct positive direction, your root must be optimism. You must first decide that you are going to manufacture optimism into every future moment of your life. A tough task, but you can do it. I will help you with techniques, so you don't shit yourself.

The Red Ball of Optimism

Imagine the feeling of optimism is actually an object, and not a feeling anymore. Why objectify optimism? Manufacturing optimism in every future moment of your life is challenging, and by boiling it down to a physical object, you are simplifying a complicated process to help rewire your emotional brain towards permanent optimism. Picture one of those little stress balls (sometimes they're red, sometimes they're shaped like small animals with eyes that bulge out when you squeeze them). Let's imagine a round, red stress ball. This stress ball is a representation of your state of thinking.

When you're in a negative state of thinking, you squeeze the ball tightly. It becomes small and shriveled. Just like your body. You slouch your shoulders, lean forward, or scowl your face, and the ball compresses with you. The longer your negative thinking remains, the harder it is for the ball to retract into its fuller state. Negative feelings are "sticky" in that way. They are harder to get away from than positive emotions.

Only optimism and positive expectations keep the ball full and expanded. Only optimism and positive expectations keep your posture tall and robust. You need that positive power to continue moving correctly - steady and secure. Think about how much energy goes into a negative feeling. High-intensity emotions wear us out. They are physically and emotionally draining. And negative emotions can have a more significant effect on us than positive ones, especially in high intensity.

This red ball is always there. By objectifying the feeling of optimism, we allow ourselves to focus on staying physically balanced in every moment. Our method will help your brain reprogram happiness receptors that will teach your intelligence (rational brain) to lead to positive emotions. Using the Red Ball of Optimism to focus on optimism is easy. Negative thoughts are sticky; happy thoughts are light and fluid. Keep your positive ball full and powered and lead with optimism.

Getting to Change

What is it? Change is not just a buzzword for the resume. Change is progress, action, opportunity, flexibility, possibility, discovery, growth, and adventure. It's also scary and uncomfortable. Here lies the challenge. Are you up for it? Grab a sheet of paper and make four sections.

Start simple. In the first section, write down 3-4 key positive labels you might use to self-identify yourself. You might write: *adventurous, hardworking and creative*. Now, in the same section, I want you to write three negative attributes you have. These can be words like *shy, quiet, and aggressive.* Now, replace the minimizing, diminutive, or limiting words with more positive words where needed. For example, you can replace the word "shy" with something like "inquisitive," "quiet" with the word "thoughtful" and "aggressive" with the word "ambitious." Never give yourself a reductive label. But it's never that simple. This activity is the concept of declaring change and igniting actionable change that sustains.

To sustain the change, you need to identify the reasons that your current state isn't working. Make a list in the second section of your paper. You can answer some of the following questions, and others that you think of yourself. Are you aligned with your career goals? Is the company you work for representing the professional purpose that aligns with yours? What are you spending your time on that isn't moving you closer to your goals? What are your blind spots? What is your performance like at work and home? Are your relationships on good terms?

This is an important part of the process. If your list reveals more reasons to change than not, you have a higher ability to transform and sustain a long-term positive change. By identifying the aspects of your life that aren't working, you can remove the limitations of your personal growth that are preventing you from achieving your goals.

In the third section of the paper, I want you to write down a list of questions and answers that describe your ideal future. What do you want to be? Where do you want to be? What is your dream job? Describe the best version of yourself. Look back at your list in section two. What can you change from that list to make a better future for yourself? You can even draw a picture if that helps.

Now you have a vision of what needs to change, and what those changes will look like. But change requires action. A vision without a roadmap is nothing. The world is filled with "idea" people. What the world lacks are those who plan and take action. Stay accountable to yourself first, then others.

In the final section of your paper, write down some actionable items and associate a time frame for each one. List what you are going to do today, tomorrow, next week, next month, next year. Make it real. This is the to-do list for your goals; it's a big deal.

Failing to change is common. But be extraordinary. I was once a four-time college dropout, but now I am a professor. Goals, hard work, persistence. To really enact extreme personal change, you have to prepare, manage, and reinforce your change. Address your resistance and identify the root causes. Engage with others for advice. Be strong. The opposition to change can't be higher than all the other parts. Otherwise, you won't change.

Every Moment is a Chance to Change Your Beliefs

How hard I try is equal to how much confidence I have in myself (and my goals). How do I know what to work on if I have no intentions or goals? Turning your expectations into written goals takes time. Formalize them. It's the fastest way to enact change in your life. Celebrate your achievements. Writing your goals is how you gain strategic advantages in your life. The world needs more planners. More strategists. More strategic leaders. Ask any CEO if they drifted through life letting things happen to them, or if they had a plan. I think you know the answer here. It's obvious, right? Leaders are thinkers and planners.

Destination Destiny

The universe doesn't care about you, me, or anyone. It doesn't care about making things happen for you. Look up at the stars and ask them your purpose tonight. Sounds silly because it is silly. We are but a tiny little speck on this planet in an even smaller speck of time. The only way you can maximize your life is by creating your happiness and building positive relationships. Living in the moment and changing the now is all you have to do to gain this fulfillment. Being a happy person with positive connections is much better than hoping and wishing for some fateful dream to come true. Shitty leaders aren't shitty on purpose. They just lack the focus to live in the moment, plan ahead, and imitate great leaders. No billionaire in a Bentley is going to stop by and hand you the keys to drive off into the Kingdom of Success. But we are what we think. Anything is within your control. Beliefs are not self-limiting. If I'm in control, I don't complain. I plan and start achieving my goals.

Written Ambition

Writing down your goals increases your propensity to achieve them. Be repetitive on purpose. Write down your goals and the reasons for each one. Three years ago, I added, "get a boat" to my list of goals because I want my child to grow up with a sense of adventure and discipline. I think that being on the sea in a sailboat will offer many opportunities for training, focus, strength, safety, and fun. When I wrote down the boat goal, I wrote down the kind of boat I want, the color of the boat, some of the details on the boat, and most importantly, why I wanted it. The more I pictured this goal and reminded myself of it daily, the closer I got to achieving this goal. The more I refine my goals, the easier it is to generate optimism about my future. And I'm now the proud owner of a red sailboat, *The Ondine.* You can catch me sailing that red beauty around San Francisco. Feel free to call me "Captain" from here on out. Captain's log, entry one: I freakin' love sailing.

This is a silly example, but you can think of how this works in your own life, and I encourage you to take a few minutes to write down your goals. I email them to myself and reply to that email 4-5 times per week (in the morning so I'll have them in mind all day). Repeating my goals over and over is the best way to make them concrete and vivid in my mind. If anyone asks for my one-year, two-year, five-year, ten-year, or lifelong goals, I'm ready to authoritatively dictate them on the spot. They are a part of me. They help maintain my optimism to enact positive changes. I don't like sharing all of my goals, though. So if you do ask me, I'll share the ones I love to share. Each goal is just for you. For example, the boat goal has many purposes, some private and personal, and other reasons that I share with others. I can use the boat to teach my son about safety, responsibility, and adventure. I wanted to learn something challenging that I'd never done before. I enjoy mindless handy work, and boats require a lot of that. And lastly, the boat can be a sanctuary where I can find creativity, peace, and harmony. Having a peaceful place to go is something everyone needs on a regular basis.

Mr. Butts, Sales Director
P&O Outsourcing Partners

Mr. Butts' efforts are starting to show. He realizes his mistakes and makes an effort to change them. He wasn't prepared for his first meeting. For the next meeting, he'll spend extra time preparing, so he doesn't waste his team's time. And he thinks that he should really get to know his team. So, he sets up an initiative to improve the culture around the office.

On the first Wednesday of every month, Mr. Butts hosts "Healthy Hump Day." He encourages his team members to sign up to host an activity that promotes wellness (like making a healthy snack, leading yoga or guided meditation).

His team feels more comfortable around him, now. Mr. Butts has a few goals he'd like to accomplish for himself, too. He writes one down on a sticky note and places it on his computer, so he sees it every day. "Be more organized." Sometimes when he sees the sticky note, he tidies up his desk a bit.

Mr. Butts is taking small steps towards important changes that make him feel better about himself.

Set Your Clock to NOW

Winston Churchill said, "no one should waste a day." Time is the most valuable form of currency, and you must be careful with how you spend it. Being wasteful with your time, spreading it thinly across tasks and giving it to people who will not pay you back will make your spirit very poor. You might as well hop in the toilet and flush your life down there where all the other waste goes.

We started with storytelling because it's a powerful way to generate influence as a leader in any given moment if you have the skills to tell the right stories, the right way. To truly connect emotionally, you need to live in the now - freely give people your best state of mind. To do that, we're going to have to deconstruct our thinking a bit.

Escape time completely. The easiest way to gain mindfulness and clarity? Nature and meditation. These two activities are proven to boost energy, reduce depression, enhance health, lower blood and heart pressures, and significantly reduce stress hormones. By escaping technology, quiet relaxation is the key to personal clarity and focus. Don't be scared of the word "meditation." It can be anything, and different for everyone. Find your form of personal meditation. It can be calm walking, sitting and staring at the waves, or lying down with your eyes closed. No need to become overwhelmed by any preconceived thoughts around what meditation is.

Time Has Wings

Let's be honest. Time doesn't fly when you're having fun - it flies no matter what you're doing. If you let yourself be the villain of the story here like Mr. Butts, then you'll just make your time fly away or worse, slip away slowly. If you've ever told someone (or yourself) that you're too busy, break down the reason behind why you're too busy. Here's an example: I'm too busy to go to the gym. Total bullsh-t. You have internal expectations to stay in shape and be healthy, but you're too busy for the gym? Are you spending so much time obliging the needs of others that you don't have time for your health? Why are you obliged to others? Why aren't you obliged to yourself? Why are the needs of other people more important than your needs?

I'm never too busy with anything because I control my life. If I can't travel to Los Angeles to see my family around the holidays, I don't say, "sorry, I'm too busy." I explain to my family their importance to me, followed by the choices and reasons I have for staying home for the holidays. And then I make plans to see them shortly after the holidays instead.

When it comes down to what's important to you, it's perfectly fine to be selfish. Being selfish often has a negative connotation, but you must put yourself, your wellbeing, and your positive framework before others. Because if you don't have those things yourself, you're not committing your best self to others, anyway.

Children Don't Need Hindsight, Why Do We?

The undeveloped and untainted mind of a child can be quite inspiring. They say funny things, but also have innocent intentions that allow them to explore the world without prejudice. In this way, they are great leaders from the start. What else does a child do?

Before having the ability to walk, they try to stand up repeatedly until they reach complete exhaustion. They play with other children regardless of status, race, clothing brands, parents, religion, incontinence, drool, etc. They prefer laughter. They keep an open mind and are curious about everything and anything. Boundaries don't exist. They are not burdened with materialism - they don't care about money, but instead care about family, friends, food, and fun. Children are primal like dogs in the morning - the first thing they do when they wake up is stretch out and look around at the world. They are simple, driven by happiness and nothing else. Children are vulnerable, seeking help often.

These qualities are innate as children, and still present within us. In some ways, we need our minds to de-evolve to become great leaders. We must find the parts of our character that were once at the forefront.

Focus on the Now: Have the End in Mind

I have this one friend, Mike, who eats like a first-year college student. Simple. Easy. Fast. Things like fast-food burgers and mac-n-cheese. But for some reason, he loves when I make him an artisanal cheese and jam plate, with cheeses from the good part of the grocery store and the expensive crackers. After a few alcoholic beverages one particular evening, I ask him if he'd like me to put together my famous cheese plate. Of course, he says, "yes, please!" I get started on my masterpiece.

I slice the harder cheeses into perfect little squares. I center them onto those fancy crackers, dab a small dollop of fig jam on top creating what I call a "three laya cracka snacka." I arrange each on the plate into the shape of a flower and sprinkle trail mix into the empty spaces. I finish the dish off with an elegant touch of finely grated cheese. One of the crackers is out of place, so I hurry to fix it. This one just won't fit right, so I eat it and arrange the rest back into a flower formation. "Damn, that's tasty." My friend salivates like a Pavlovian dog once he hears the plate lift from the kitchen tabletop, recalling the last time I took him to Flavortown with my cracka snackas. I am immediately happy with the result of my hard work. But wait! I go back to the kitchen and hustle the items back to the fridge so I can join the party and am quickly jolted into a state of panic. There's a massive layer of mold on the underside of the jam jar. "Noooooo!" I yell at my friend to stop eating the crackers. Luckily, he's still admiring my work of art and hasn't eaten one, yet. My stomach starts to twist and turn when I realize something. Oh crap - I ate one.

I'm at a standoff with the moldy lid, staring and wondering what will happen to me. Will I puke? Maybe. Will the mold grow inside of me, birthing tiny, moldy, fig-jam beings? Probably.

How did I forget to check the moldy lid? Because nobody checks the lid, ever! Sometimes you get so caught up in the now, building your cheese plate, that you forget to check the quality of your ingredients and the image of a perfect ending. So sometimes you mess up and eat moldy jam, but at least you realized before you served it to everyone else. Next time I am in the market, I will get a new jam.

The significance of this story? Planning. You don't want to ever waste your time and efforts because of something you could have fixed earlier. Planning is underrated. If you've ever shown up to a meeting unprepared, you know what happens. Nothing gets accomplished, and several people just wasted an hour ruffling through a meeting that could have taken 15 minutes, or "should have been an email." Preparedness shows that you respect your team and care about the time of everyone involved. Planning is important. If you don't, sometimes you end up wasting people's time, and sometimes you end up eating moldy jam.

Pièce de Résistance

In summary, we have to recognize everything within our self-control. Our attitude (including the ability to laugh), our ability to change and the way we spend our time. These are all within our self-control. We must remember to laugh, manufacture optimism, live in the now and write down our goals. Each of these factors dictates how we enact change in our lives, and it is important to acknowledge both our resistance to vulnerability or things that make us uncomfortable, and ultimately our resistance to change.

Mr. Butts, VP of Sales
P&O Outsourcing Partners

Mr. Butts stands in his decisive black attire with the team at P.O.O.P. for the announcement of his new title: VP of Sales.

Wow, he has come a long way! And his team is happy for him. He accepts his promotion with a proud, humble grin. He looks to his team to declare his gratitude. No notecards this time. Instead, he tells them a story.

"Once when I was fighting with my brothers, my grandfather told us to stop fighting, to go outside and collect sticks and return with a bundle. When we came back with a pile, he told us to break each stick into two pieces. We did it with ease. He urged us to go back out and grab another bundle. But this time we had to break the sticks as a bundle, not individually. We were dumbfounded when we couldn't snap the bundle whole. My grandfather saw us struggling with the bundle and said, 'You see? Individually the sticks are easy to break but united; they are too powerful.'"

Mr. Butts' vision is for a brighter future, without poor communication and laziness, sadness or boredom. One without shitty leadership. And he's going to ensure that vision is a reality at P.O.O.P.

LEAD THE FUTURE

Shitless GOATs

The Super Tribe

Leadership takes practice because it is a journey and developed over many years. You don't become the *greatest of all time* (GOAT) without years of failure and self-reflection. It also requires Shitsuke (a Japanese word for hard work, training, and discipline).

We *shat down* to interview the most successful and innovative leaders we could find. These global leaders were happy to share their secrets and stories about their road to success. Even better, they've worked at some of the most successful organizations, including a restaurant chain backed by a *Shark* investor. We also interviewed a college president. Woah.

Why Study Leaders?

We study leaders because we all work and want a livable wage, at the very least. But on the road to glory, we get into shitty positions where our bosses suck, or maybe you are the boss, and every time you open your mouth, your team is reminded of the last time they "negotiated the release of some chocolate hostages."

We often read articles and books that inspire us so we can get our dream job. We want to develop new skills. We seek them out. And you'll learn new skills from our hand-picked batch of leaders. You will learn how their genius will increase your awareness of the world and help you get closer to your goals. Their behaviors, knowledge, values, and ideas have changed me. We, like chimps, pass on the most useful parts of our culture through a personal and societal connection. Here I am passing along all of the tips I've learned from the best people I know, like a handsome little chimp.

The continuous journey of self-improvement keeps us wanting more. We seek to inspire others and relish in the success of our peers, a behavior that leaders share. When will things get better? When will I be the leader?

Why become a leader? In the global marketplace with highly mature and saturated industries, only invisible opportunities remain. To identify and engage in these opportunities, it takes a new kind of leader. That's what I want to be. A collaborative and strategic visionary with expertise in economics and psychology. An adaptive transformational artist of commerce that bridges the gap between creativity and execution, threat and opportunity. This type of person is rare, but they become this way through deliberate personal development. For that reason - nothing is keeping any of us from becoming the next future-proof leader.

This idea ignited my passion for developing a leadership book and for improving the effectiveness of organizational leadership through the practical application of simple business concepts.

We believe that our "super tribe" of leaders behave in extraordinarily particular and distinctly purposeful ways by developing a personal catalog of inspiration-driving behaviors.

They get you to *want to do* what they want. This is different from motivation, which is just getting you *to do* what they want. Linking behaviors to desired feelings are the key here. Example: I do something, it increases my influence, so I keep doing it. And it's not a simple list of 5-10 practice points. It's hundreds of behavioral practices. This is an essential part of the book, so let's jump in.

Leaders We Love

Alexander the Great!

Alex is our all-time favorite foodie entrepreneur, and we were lucky enough to get a little taste of his leadership. He is responsible for one of the most excellent new food concepts of the decade. His recipe for success is *al dente*, tender but firm. His advice is like nothing you've heard before and contradicts most business books.

Do you have a friend that you're proud of? Alex is that guy for me. He is my long-time friend and mentor that I met way back in the 7th grade (Spartan Marching Band!). I consider myself to be a leader and a lot of my development comes from lessons I learned from Alex over the years (especially in the last five years). During childhood, he was a leader in our school band and drumline. Now he is the CEO/founder of an American-Chinese food enterprise with stakes from the best investors on the planet (literally - if you think of the top four most notable investors in the world, *at least* one of them has backed Alex. No joke).

Our discussion started just after he landed at LAX from China. We talked for hours about his business. The topic of leadership philosophy and modern business excites us; once you get us going, it's hard to make us stop.

After a rigorous academic path culminating in advanced business degrees from top schools, Alex went on to a successful corporate career in the US and China. A multitude of thrilling projects crossed his desk. One day, he decided to jump all in and leave the desk job.

You could title his backstory section, "Stepping into the Unknown," because that's what happened. Back in the summer of 2015, Alex came up with a brand new fusion food concept that he thought would be a hit in the Chinese market. He had over a decade of experience as an investor and consultant when the idea hit him. He immediately went to work in his kitchen in Beijing and began laying the groundwork for a new potential business, even though he was treating it as just a pet project. After he threw together a simple logo, he created an Instagram account which bombastically (and somewhat facetiously) read: "Coming in 2016 to Los Angeles, New York, Beijing, and Shanghai." It turned out he got one of the four cities right. After convincing one of his friends to join him in the effort to start up a new business, he immediately flew to China from his home in LA, not knowing what to expect or when he would return.

Alex and his new partner, a Harvard-educated business person and restaurant owner, immediately got to work. Within a month, they had perfected the recipes and began testing the concept at a few pop-up events. An investment offer came in almost immediately. It was almost too easy. "Boom, happy times," they said this as they sipped beers and took tequila shots on a lovely restaurant patio in Beijing's Sanlitun party district. They took the cash and got to work in the Fall of 2016. They developed an elegant brand, formed their corporate entity, went to bigger and better events where their fusion food concept entirely crushed it and had just enough to money start their own food delivery business. Happy times they were. Until they weren't.

Fight or Flight

Three months into the new delivery business venture, Alex and his partner realized they would run out of cash within six weeks. The weight of delays, massive rents, and being a new food and beverage concept without mass market traction had led to much higher burn rates than either partner had anticipated. Worse, the two were finding the climate for new investment to be much more challenging than their chance experience over the prior summer. In China, labor law dictates that employees are entitled to one month of severance pay when terminated, meaning the business had two weeks to either find more capital or cease operating. Alex and his partner, having not taken salaries the prior nine months, were in no position to continue funding the business on their own. Alex's options as CEO looked pretty bleak. Without positive cash flow, the investors they had approached – no less than 80 – were smelling blood and not touching the business.

Now, he faced the choice: fight or flight. Alone in his Beijing apartment on a cold Friday night in January, Alex began lobbing bombs. Old friends, former employers, venture capitalists he didn't know, people on LinkedIn he found who looked like they might have money, even some of his customers... Alex started firing off emails. One-by-one he tried to find a white knight, still holding onto some wish that his business would grow the legs it needed to make it through its bad times and get back into some "happy times." One person responded. This one just happened to be a billionaire and one of the most famous investors in the United States. Alex found his email address in a forum on Quora and wrote to him directly. To his shock, he got a reply. The investor's assistant happened to have a Beijing visit planned for the following month and wanted to see the business and meet Alex. At this time, the decision was made to stay on course, at the risk of incurring significant personal debt to cover overhead. Despite high monthly burn, the brand became too endeared to too many customers in Beijing. Alex knew he had a great product and a great brand and was not willing to throw in the towel.

Sure enough, the meeting went beautifully. Alex carefully told his story and elucidated on why his fusion concept was potentially explosive. Soon after, the investor's assistant emailed Alex stating the business was not yet mature enough to justify an investment. This was after Alex, and his partner decided to keep operating at the risk of incurring liabilities they could not repay. Rejection is a big part of the business, and not only had Alex and his partner experienced their share of it, but they were on the cusp of severe failure and personal burnout.

Like in baseball, sometimes you gotta hit singles and try to get on base. The series of letdowns made Alex and his partner more focused. Rather than swinging for the fences, they aimed for small incremental, wins. Their prior investors took note of their sacrifice and threw them a bone. A little bridge round of investment was needed to allow them time to find more outside funding. It gave them just enough time to find a better location, which would reduce their overhead and increase their nightly revenues. They moved, and soon enough the business was at a comfortable breakeven. They were no longer flooding out cash and instead were able to apply their bridge funding toward developing factory production, which they knew could be a game changer.

Around this time, the media community took note of Alex's business, and a few video and print interviews about his fusion food concept had gone viral. Persevering led to some small breaks. The series of little wins eventually led to a break. That famous US investor? Word got back to his team that Alex's business successfully stabilized itself and was taking steps toward factory mass production. The investor saw the grit that it required to stay alive and move the ball down the field into a more scalable food business. By the summer of 2017, Alex and his partner had an investment term sheet. With all else failing, they found a way to win. At the time of this writing, Alex and his partner have successfully closed their deal and are taking significant orders from major Chinese retailers. Happy times, you could say.

What are the big lessons here? Failure is a prerequisite, just like you hear from Michael Jordan and Mike Tyson when they talk about athletic successes. To dominate their respective sport, they failed more than anyone else. Mike Tyson once said, "Everybody has a plan until they get punched in the face."

How to Inspire?

So, we know how Alex built his brand and gained success. But how does Alex inspire people as a leader? Where does the motivation come from? It's easy.

Overpayment results in overachievement. Alex deliberately overpays his staff. By taking a higher risk on the people that are newly on-boarded, you won't have to worry about getting their best. He told me about a brilliant young woman that just started. She had a college degree, and her values matched his, so he paid her double what she would get anywhere else and now she is killin' it. Loyal as anyone could ask for and works twice as hard as anyone else. Usually, employers post a salary range and try to get the best person in that range. Alex does the opposite. He posts precisely what he is looking for, and then pays the person according to their value to the company. As a result, his company is full of *awesome*.

Personal habits should be unapologetic if they help the business. The next golden nugget of advice from Alex is his view of a typical misconception about successful entrepreneurs and their daily hours. There have been studies about Fortune 500 CEO-tendencies and their commonalities, like 4 AM wake-up call, gym, newspaper, reflection, meditation. But like Winston Churchill, Alex likes to work late and take his sweet-ass time waking up in the morning. Even during World War II, Churchill would lie in bed until noon, or close to it. Don't feel bad, either. It's cool if you want to be a night owl. He rolls up like that because he likes to "bat cleanup." This is baseball language for a grand slam, offensive-type batter that comes in late to sweep up the bases and score big. By arriving later, Alex can take stock of everything that has happened over the course of the day, evaluate, and provide reliable feedback to address the *shit* that's gone awry. Alex is a notoriously *4-5 AM-er* like Churchill. Alex works every waking hour; the hours are merely untraditional (like most of Alex's story). In the wee hours of the morning, he can also tee-up things for tomorrow without distraction.

Communication is key. Emailing like a ninja is a useful skill to have. Contrary to popular belief, he doesn't believe emails should be short. Alex preemptively answers any possible question and includes details. Not long-winded, just carefully calculated. It's about the quality of the communication. Emails take him a long time to write because he packs them with details and plenty of explainers. That way he won't have to go back and forth with people to give them the information he already knew that they might need. It's easy to anticipate what they're going to ask and answer it in advance.

A couple of years ago, when I invited someone onto the Board of Directors of my previous company, Alex told me to send the board members updates, news, and relevant info, periodically, showing them what's current. The first few I sent to Alex first, and he helped me craft them like a genius. I have used this approach in my daily emails ever since. By reducing needless and mindless back-and-forth nonsense, people can recognize you as a quality communicator. This works in presentations, too. Just know your audience, see the person your sending information to and what they want out of it.

Positive feedback and compliments shouldn't be cheap. With input and other company direction, the conviction is a must. Demonstrate it. Have great belief in anything you say. Words matter. Saying "good job" must be the real deal. If you say it all the time, you cheapen it like dirt. And your team will be wise to how invaluable your word is if you shell-out compliments to anyone, with no real meaning. It's good advice. Don't lose the validity of conviction or credibility. Be real, dude.

The buck stops here! The unique value? Plain grit. As you have seen in the company's backstory, there were many chances to call it quits. But no. He sucked it up and persisted. People don't know this about the business, but the best are the best because they fail the most and keep going. Leaders have to stick with the conviction and the grit. Do the work. Have faith in yourself and people; it will save you. Even though it took Alex a year and a half, the long road to cash generation was worth the effort. Every successful business person will tell you about the many times their business almost failed. The CEO must take responsibility and build momentum.

The Journey

What's next for Alex? A lot of companies like his get bought out after 5-10 years. Understanding that the shelf life of an independent food company isn't everlasting, I was interested to know what his future held. He discussed how focused he is in the business today and the importance of demonstrating "stickiness" that'll build major revenues. On the long road to get a joint venture or buyout, there will be many more failures and lessons learned. These lessons can help others, so Alex wants to go back to work in private equity and venture capital as an advisor to businesses going through similar journeys in consumer or food and beverage companies (in China). He feels that this is where his value to the economy lies and I agree with him, especially since he has advised me on business and I know firsthand what that experience is like. The future brings him back to his purpose: maximizing business efforts by supporting entrepreneurs. Said alternatively, "helping others."

Alex can do these things with the set of skills required to create influence, inspiration, and change. If you're lucky, you may meet a few rare people like Alex in your lifetime.

Next, we want to know what imitable behavior he uses to support those methods so we can learn to use them in our day-to-day leadership.

Soup Without Bouillon is Just Hot Water

"Alex, so what's your secret sauce?" How do you add that extra bit of flavor to your work? He trusts his staff, so he tells them face-to-face that he believes in them, but mostly (95%) through his actions. He focuses on making them feel trusted so that they can utilize their autonomy to make the best possible business decisions and achieve higher job performance and personal job satisfaction.

Alex's specific behaviors that evoke trust:

1. Alex listens without interrupting and asks for reasons. He asks questions and digs into the details while looking you in the eyes. Alex may or may not take your advice, but he listens to your thoughts, asks for an explanation and reasoning, and treats you and your opinions with respect. Alex doesn't lead by consensus; he makes the decisions. But either way, you can expect to be heard if you work for Alex. He also doesn't push a decision down the chain without providing logic, purpose, and clear expectations.
2. He delegates responsibility for the comparable amount of authority needed. These behaviors create opportunities that support autonomous staff decision-making. Alex steers the vessel towards glory, but he doesn't tell the chef how to cut the carrots down in the galley. He gives the chef room to breathe and figure it out.
3. He gives candid feedback. None of that mushy sandwich (good news, then bad news, then good news) stuff. If you crush it, he will let you know. And you'll love it because his "atta boy" pat on the back feels good. Alex is good at making you see where you stand. But if you bushwhack it, get ready for a sit-down with open ears.
4. New ideas are accepted, encouraged, and implemented to promote change within the culture.

5. Walking meetings keep the momentum flowing and it makes you feel like you are going somewhere with Alex. Travel the journey together.

Other leadership tips from Alex:

1. Repeat questions and answers for clarity if you don't understand 100%.
2. Be calm under pressure and make sure the team knows you have their back.
3. Take the time to give positive praise in public when they deserve it and discuss development in private (investing in people).

People crave power to find autonomy to make their own decisions. Give them the power and let them see their potential. The freedom of self-direction is priceless, so give your employees the space to become incredible. That's what Alex does. He has executed specific behaviors to elicit feelings of trust that enable autonomy. When used genuinely, it is a useful tool for leading high performing teams.

Let's do a visualization: how does your favorite boss make you feel and what behaviors can you perform that will elicit those types of desired feelings and responses? This is the way Alex figures out how to act. He'll ask himself, "how did they make me feel so important? What behaviors did they use?" Then he will use those behaviors to make others feel important. Alex is cognizant of others and how they behave.

Alex created a product for the largest market in the world by integrating two cultures and cuisines into a food fusion. Economically speaking, he found an invisible opportunity that other restaurateurs never saw. It's his fierce creativity, persistent passion, and grit that turned his idea into reality. This wasn't his first business, though. He tried his hand in several industries before getting into food.

Alex, to many people, can come off a little harsh because of his candid style. If you know his intent, it's okay because you can understand what he is doing with tough love. But sensitive people don't do well with this, and Alex has found himself struggling there, making changes to his approach so that he is still harsh and real, but not burning bridges. Critiquing with a smile is one way.

Happiness and emotions? Alex is a happy person. His friends describe him as someone who laughs a lot and is always a blast to be around. He is well-regulated, showing restraint and discipline in his behaviors. Although I've never seen him angry, he admits to getting frustrated. But he controls his emotions using self-esteem and emotional intelligence.

Final tips from Alex:

1. Your vision must connect to people and align in every part of the business.
2. Have the tough conversations that require courage.
3. Do what you say you're going to do and don't waste time (if you could have the meeting today instead of tomorrow, do it now).
4. Prove to investors that you can make money.

The global economy relies on leaders like Alex who play a vital role in the development of others, building the economy from scratch. The most successful future-proof leaders must be keenly aware of the sensitivity of other people while remaining passionate and enduring to the importance of transforming, improving, and evolving. Effective leaders must exude confidence from excellence. They must identify the problem that destroys opportunities for people in our generation and the future, and then present a solution. Alex created a business by connecting people to a shared culture and innovative cuisine. Transform your future using his virtuous leadership techniques.

Laura the Explora

Laura is our favorite expert in global leadership development. Why global? How is it different from the regular version? Think of it as *extreme leadership*. Like the difference between skateboarding on the streets and Tony Hawk skateboarding on a vertical ramp at the X Games. It's a lot more challenging to lead a multinational organization than a domestic one. And this requires a new kind of global expert that can communicate across cultures and borders. Laura has dedicated her entire professional career to improving global leadership with companies like PG&E (energy) and Kaiser Permanente (healthcare).

In addition to the $87 million PG&E development initiative which received praise from the White House, her current role at Kaiser Permanente will be the career challenge of a lifetime. How can leaders in healthcare change the industry once and for all? Damn, nobody can answer that. But Laura is well on her way.

"Discovery, exploration, and inspiration" are her buzz words. She is the most active thinker I know and the most cultured traveler. She sonders around the globe into the nooks and crannies of Nepal, India, Israel, Belize, and the likes. Her secret to personal success: develop expertise in a field that you are passionate about so you can help others and make a positive impact on the world. And you may need to travel the world to do so.

If you've ever been excited about an upcoming vacation, you may know the feeling of *resfeber*. It's the heart-racing excitement of your anticipated journey ahead. Laura lives in this atmosphere because an international trip is always weeks away. She isn't eager to get away, though. It's not an ecophobic "I gotta leave home or work" mentality, believing she has to get away from it all like a roaming vagrant. Laura yearns to immerse herself in new cultures, finding the best ways to help others. She seeks to understand what life on the rest of our planet is like because it informs the way she helps other leaders develop the best practices. It's the healing way of Shinrin-Yoku, the medicine of being in nature and bathing in the forest of life. Not all who wander are lost, and not all who wander lust. Laura has a sense of "wonder" versus a sense of "wander." This idea drives her spiritual-like thirst for knowledge.

Wanting to experience the world in a quaquaversal direction, Laura once spun a desktop globe and stopped it with her finger to choose her next destination. No re-spinnies! Even if she landed on Boring, Oregon (it's a real place) that's where she was headed. I double-dog dare you to try. It takes guts to commit to that. Commitment to the unknown is a quality only the most skilled leader (and entrepreneur) has acquired in their toolbox. Traveling more and immersing herself in different places has her much more comfortable to take risks that matter. The other benefit of world travel? Learning how to manage ambiguity, an essential skill for leaders.

Besides traveling to unknown destinations, Laura is the queen of *dérive*. That's when the only guide to a journey is the spontaneous adventure. No planned zip-lining or scuba lessons. If it happens organically by stumbling into it, sign her up that moment because she will try it all. Just ask her about the time she jumped onto a catamaran off the Placencia Peninsula in Belize during storm season (ok, fine, it wasn't storm season).

Flying Towards Fear

Laura profoundly loves life, takes a sincere interest in her passions, and has an awareness of the universe. It's not through expansive knowledge, but a simple understanding that the unknown is vast and distant travel experience has value. Laura has had so many compelling chance encounters in various countries that she believes in the wonder and greatness of people. Her career in leadership development reflects that passion for helping others along with her career path. Example, many of her travels were fueled by charitable need, whether it was working with nonprofits to develop their leadership, to helping educators in the slums of India and working with refugee leaders in Israel.

Some words can lock us into negative judgments. "Strange" often has a negative connotation. Not to Laura. Her state of happiness and prosperity originates from her ability to understand things at their root. This includes positivity and resiliency. It's important when traveling and communicating across cultures, both verbally and with your body language. Riding the voyage of global leadership, Laura now serves the leadership development community in California, helping top companies bolster effectiveness, strengthen talent pipelines and develop a best-in-class brand. She designs her programs to prepare leaders for the challenges of tomorrow, anywhere around the globe.

The Road Less Traveled is Less Traveled for a Reason

Years back while attending UC Berkeley's Executive Coaching Program, Laura expected to learn about frameworks and tools, perhaps even role-model a coaching framework. But what she didn't expect, is that the program would focus on learning about herself, at the deepest level. After revealing her most personal stories, darkest fears, individual failures, and insecurities, Laura eventually discovered her path to achieving her dreams. Through the tremendously detailed self-reflection, she was able to uncover things which had been holding her back. She realized the power and vulnerability of achieving purpose in life. It has since helped her fully connect with other people, develop stronger relationships, and see the sea of unlimited possibilities. As you are reading this, think of your insecurities. Are they holding you back? For me, one thing I've been extraordinarily insecure about was my neck. I often avoided meetings in person because I didn't want to have to explain to everyone why my neck was stiff. Over time though, I challenged this insecurity and tried to embrace it the way Laura advised me to. These days, I don't even think about it.

One of Laura's most significant struggles in leadership was not knowing what kind of leader to be. She watches others, aware of how they show up, how they interact and what makes them great. There is not one type of leader, but there are different styles of leadership to achieve mixed results. For some people, they may subscribe to a specific theory, such as transformational leadership. Laura seeks to understand what others value, especially when joining a new environment. Her leadership style is quite adaptive.

The road to successful leadership is not paved with gold. Laura has taken on projects that didn't work out, she has been in places she did not like, and she sure as hell felt alone many times along the way. Laura told me, "It's ok to be scared. It's ok to fail. We're human after all and success is always on the other side of failure."

Leadership Tips from Laura:

1. Constantly seek feedback to improve.
2. Listen first because people want to be understood, respected and cared for.
3. Work gets done through relationships; nothing can substitute that.
4. Be authentic, modeling the behaviors of your best self.
5. Action without purpose is not useful.
6. Real leadership requires high emotional intelligence.
7. Take time to watch other leaders you want to be like.
8. Show up 100%, no half-ass attempts.
9. Seek excellence in a lifetime pursuit.

So let's circle back. Laura has a task to fix the impossible: fix healthcare by improving a nearly 100-year-old company. At least we know one thing, they picked the right person for the job. Her travels have given her the resiliency for anything. She is positive, focused, flexible, proactive and an all-around good human.

Her final suggestions, listen close:

1. Positivity: resilient people are optimists. They display self-assurance based on their view that life is complicated but filled with opportunities.
2. Focus: this characteristic of resilient people reflects having a clear vision. Visualize yourself one year from now after making a transition towards your vision.
3. Be proactive: engage change rather than defend against it.

The Ring-Leading Lip Reader from Higher Education

This next story is about Jeff, the college president at Lake Tahoe Community College, and the author of the foreword of this book. He is a leader in all his roles; father, soccer coach, friend, brother, son, and college president. You might call him a "natural-born" leader? No. No. No.

If you ever met someone and thought they were a "natural-born" leader, think again. They don't exist! People are not born with the ability to lead (trait theory). People are not born with intelligence or confidence. These skills come from your cognitive domain, not from your childhood or birth. Your cognitive skills develop through training and education. These so-called "natural-born" leaders appear to be organic in their leadership because their behaviors are genuine and purposeful. They also don't push their visions using positional power. They use the connection, compassion, and social influence.

As a college president (in fact, he is the youngest community college president in California's history), Jeff's leadership exudes purpose and relational trust. He is a modern-day George Washington, a complete underdog (because of his age) that rose to the highest position at his organization while still in his thirties.

At colleges, resources are always a top concern. Leading through a lack of budget is a lot harder than a high-margin pharmaceutical company, for example.

The section title is *Ring-Leading Lip Reader.* That's because when I first met Jeff, I thought he was deaf. He stared at my face as if he was reading my lips. I'd never met someone who listens so closely. He leads with his ears. Also, he looks like a president and is exceptionally well-dressed. Not flashy, just clean and crisp. Two minutes into meeting him, I wanted to be just like him.

The other day when a voicemail notification popped up on my phone, I noticed something. The last five voicemails I got were all from Jeff. Then I checked my call log. He was all over there too. And it's not what you're thinking. He isn't blasting me with phone calls. These were over the course of couple months. He is really good about talking through things with people instead of firing off an email. He prefers verbal and face-to-face communication. I respect that. (Also, I realized that Jeff and I have talked on the phone more than I've talked to my mom. Yikes, time to call mom.)

I have been impressed with Jeff, mainly because I hadn't looked at higher education as the place to find global leaders. It's no surprise that he is highly educated as a college president, but can he offer any advice to folks outside of academia? Yes, and then some. Education does not guarantee success as a leader. Nor am I implying that leaders without formal training are disadvantaged or ill-equipped. But Jeff is crushing it.

Tips from Jeff:

1. Servant leaders have an intrinsic purpose: helping others, community, and youth (this translates into business settings as well).
2. Be a part of something bigger than yourself.

3. Practice mental toughness, long-term dedication, and perseverance to goals.
4. Never give up on yourself or your dreams, just make a plan and do it.

Lead by Example

Jeff once told me that "Public education is the great equalizer," and that is why he devotes his professional life to "ensuring students achieve their academic, professional, and personal goals with community college playing a critical role as a pathway to the middle class." Additionally, "students first" is listed as his top core value. Jeff is a real role model and admirable colleague. His vision is not inward-facing or self-focused. He only wishes to better the lives of students.

WWJD = What Would Jeff Do

How does someone become a college president?" Jeff is like our other members of the "super tribe." But one thing here is quite distinct. He took his business skills into the world of higher education so he could live out his purpose. Servant leadership to the max.

"Authors are like musicians, singing their stories in pages," Jeff tells me after reading this book to prepare his foreword. "When I find authors I like, I latch on for dear life because they're not easy to find." I found this compliment to be pretty impactful for a few reasons. First, Jeff acknowledged me as an author, which I hadn't claimed before, considering this book is numero uno. Second, Jeff knows I am a musician, so he used the musical association to compliment the text. Lastly, he stated how he is committed to reading future writings. Is there a better compliment? I think not. He also complimented me on things that are within my self-control, which always feels better! So I ask myself when I get into a position where I can be influential, what would Jeff do?

New Phone, Who Dis? Brian.

Here's the last episode: the return of the author. Have you ever received a text message from someone you didn't know (or from a contact whose number you didn't save - oops) and then decided to mess with them? Damn, that's harsh. Hopefully, you came clean. Next time, just say, "new phone, who dis?" That phrase can also be used for something else, too. When you get a question you don't want to answer, you reply, "new phone, who dis?" It's equivalent to playing dumb.

This leads you to my Emotional Intelligence Game. This requires a friend.

1. Think of what animal best portrays you.
2. Call a friend or go hang out with someone.
3. Ask what animal they would use to describe you.
4. Ask "why" five times to get down to the very root of it.
5. Then tell them what animal you'd express yourself with and why.
6. Discuss the differences between your answers.
7. Then, repeat the same exercise with you choosing their animal.

Now that you've played the game, think about the following questions:

1. How did it feel to be called an animal that you didn't select?
2. Did you choose a "cooler" animal for yourself than they assigned to you? What does that say about you? Them?
3. Are you unhappy with how this turned out? Or did it become a fun conversation with your friend or whoever you played with?
4. What was your emotional state before, during, and after playing the game?

5. What are the differences between the animal you selected for yourself and what the other person chose?

I've played this with my family, friends, and coworkers. The point of the game is to review your emotions in a situation that requires strange answers. Being called a "dog" instead of a "lion" shouldn't upset you. Explore your emotions and make a mental note of what you felt during the conversation. Here's what an emotionally intelligent person would likely do:

1. Enjoy the process and make it fun.
2. Explore emotions and dig into the *why* questions.
3. Reflect on the game afterward.
4. Understand that people see you differently than you see yourself.
5. If someone calls you an armadillo when you thought you were a tiger, just say "new phone, who dis?"

I started my section off with a game because this is a critical facet of my leadership style. I believe in using relatable examples, associative thinking, and analogies. These are vital tools in making both mental and social connections. We all learn better and engage more when we draw from personal experiences that others may relate to.

Next, in memory of George Washington, USA's big poppa, I am going to make a bold declaration: leaders these days are getting off the hook way too easily. Even at the highest levels of corporate leadership, I've seen CEOs and CFOs of publicly-traded companies practicing poor leadership habits. It's the reason for this book. But it's not just in business. We are at a time where it's getting harder and harder to find good leadership examples in every setting.

Dumb question: have you ever seen your boss make the same mistake over and over again? They are squandering valuable moments of influence, saying things without thinking, making bad moves, and not acting like a leader. The moments from these leaders are the chocolate wheelie fart crumbs that create a culture of leadershit. Maybe you can't teach an old dog new tricks, but new leaders must learn how to be better than that, and that's what I strive to achieve every day, as should you.

One of the most significant turning points in my life happened when a classmate, Dan, confronted me after class one day. He said he noticed when we left class the previous week, we drove the same way on the freeway, took the same exit, and ultimately pulled into the same apartment building. I told him I already knew we lived in the same building. He asked me how long I knew, and I revealed that I knew for at least 8-10 months at that point. He was shocked and seemed betrayed, wondering why I wouldn't have told him as if I was purposefully avoiding him all those months. His puzzled and questionable face said a lot. But he was younger than me, jocky, and wore backward NY Yankee hats to class. I had made up my mind about him before I met him. I thought he was a tool, and I had no interest in becoming friends. I didn't realize the importance of this situation, but it would plague me later.

At home in silent reflection, I realized something. How could I be that kind of person? So shut-off to my classmates that I deliberately lost an opportunity to become friends with someone or potentially learn something valuable from them. I'm no leader. This was undergraduate school, in a business program. Why was I acting like this? This is a failure. It took place because of my selfishness, insecurity and antisocial behavior. Time to change. I was the tool, and ultimately an asshole.

Soon after that, Dan and I became friends in class, worked on projects together, and then hung out outside of the classroom as well. We became inseparable and even traveled to England to study abroad together at the prestigious University of Oxford. Looking back at that time in my life, I realize how grateful I am for his leadership. It was his confrontation that allowed me this BFFL relationship and individual development. He instilled confidence in me and taught me to be more social. From then on, I was determined to become someone else's leader, the way he was for me. In many ways, this book holds a lot of the lessons I learned from him. The younger, jocky toolbag I refused to be friends with now teaches me the most valuable lessons in business school. He also reminded me that people are always more interesting than they seem if you give them a chance.

My philosophy of leadership is simple:

1. Use relatable examples, associative thinking, and analogies to help people make connections.
2. Treat everyone like your best friend, Dan.
3. Act like a baby elephant with happy energy (random, but I'll explain in a moment).
4. Time is gold, don't ever disappoint your future self.
5. Always learn, change, and be the best you can be.

BFFLs

Like Dan, leaders understand that the science of trust is a simple concept. People trust those who take care of them. Trust is the opposite of self-interest. Leaders need to give. And they constantly give. Our brains are hardwired to automatically trust those who provide us with support, safety, shelter, food, and care.

How do I give support? Listen. Be open, be vulnerable, be honest. Eye contact and laughing also increase oxytocin, the physical ingredient in trust. Turn every interaction into an opportunity to give something to someone. And provide feedback. You can be someone who doesn't need something in return. You can create a safe space for connection and talk. Don't behave with actions that foster mistrust. Don't act cautious, hesitant and unsure. As with my best friend, I treat him well out of genuine care, not to get anything from him.

In England, Dan was my tour guide because he had arrived a week before me to explore the sites. When I arrived, he always asked me, "how did your tour guide get so handsome?" He is a funny, fun-loving guy and his humor comes from paying attention to people's personalities and being happy.

Be a Baby Elephant

Why don't you ever see elephants hiding in trees? Because they're so good at it! I don't know who to credit this joke to, but it's pure genius.

Baby elephants, besides being adorable, are 200-pound babies capable of uniting herds of elephants. When they are not feeling well, they rumble. And when they rumble, everyone rumbles. The entire elephant parade will come by to caress the baby elephants with their trunks. Elephants even hold community ceremonies to honor birth and death. This is the essence of being part of something bigger than ourselves. Elephants live as a supportive community, untainted by judgment. They are servants to each other. They help others before helping themselves. They have courage, compassion, and connection. I like the idea of being the baby elephant, uniting people and being part of a community that cares for each other. Did you ever think that "act like a baby elephant" would be a leadership tip?

Time

I'm genuinely excited about time because every year I lose a year. And because of that, I never waste time. Also 'cause, my Poppi told me not to! Ask my friends what I was like ten years ago and what I'm like today: nearly unrecognizable, and it's because of my use of time.

Other leadership tips from me:

1. Don't complain; you have control of that.
2. Compliment people on things within their self-control.
3. Help everyone by engaging the unengaged, kick start things - be the ignition, not the brakes.
4. There is no substitute for face-to-face relationship building.
5. Personal connections are the backbone of everything in business and life.

6. Plan and prepare, so you live the life you want, instead of falling into a career you never wanted.
7. Always be funny - don't hold in your jokes.
8. If you present an idea, provide the idea with a plan to show you thought it through.
9. Make it about them, with genuine interest. If someone brings up their kids (or anything), ask about them, don't talk about yourself unless they ask back.

Use Your Words Carefully

People watch leaders. Everything you do sends a message to someone. So use your words carefully. Here is an example. "Do Things Right" or "Do the Right Things?" Next time you tell someone that you are an "effective" person with a "good work ethic," think again. Are you? Why did you say that? What do you do that makes you capable?

Improving your efficiency means doing things right (like typing quickly). Management and tactical functions fall into this category. Work smarter, not harder. But think about this regarding your day-to-day living, not just business. Do I remain energetic and focused on my work and personal life? Do I get tasks done quickly and move on? If yes, excellent job. If no, maybe give these some thought.

Improving effectiveness means doing the right things, strategically. This is when you work ON the business and not IN the business. Again, let's step outside of the business perspective and into real life by asking some intelligent questions. Am I a critical thinker or do I accept things as they are? Why am I working in this career, for this company? Do I challenge myself to be better and learn new skills? Do I spend time in nature or feel a sense of burnout? Is my life following the path I want or do things just happen to me?

Just focus on your effectiveness first by writing down your plans and vision (strategy), then develop your efficiency by becoming more self-aware (tactical). Keep a journal for a few days, and you'll be surprised to find out where you spend your time. There's a lot of minutes in the day. Every minute is a chance to turn things around. Don't underestimate yourself. Be useful, don't just say you're "effective."

Toast This

Not bread, but Toastmasters. It's a club where you can practice your leadership, communication, and public speaking. You can always tell a Toastmaster apart from everyone else. A lot of leaders are terrible speakers, and one of my goals was to help people with public speaking, especially in a moment of influence.

Public speaking has become one of my favorite hobbies (after sailing, of course). The same way the that Jeff isn't a natural-born leader and has to work at it, public speaking is also not a natural skill. Here are my tips for success at speaking:

1. Practice. Seriously. It is obvious, but nobody does it. Join Toastmasters.
2. Remove unneeded parts from your speech (by practicing it) and always end before the maximum time allowed.
3. Informal and conversational styles are much more relatable than formal styles.
4. Is your cause worthy? What are you saying about the future? Will people care?
5. Make your energy contagious.
6. Don't write a script, use bullet points and practice off that.
7. Choose your first and final words carefully.
8. Humor is most memorable.

Tips while speaking:

1. Grab people's attention.
2. Address the audience and introduce yourself.

98

3. Summarize what the talk will be about.
4. Use intro, middle (usually three points), and conclusion format.
5. Replace filler words (um, and, so) with a pause instead. Silence is powerful.
6. Focus on one person at a time, five seconds or so, then move on to someone else.
7. Use the space you have, get away from the podium.
8. Use hand gestures above your shoulder height; this energy is more exciting.
9. When discussing emotions in your speech, walk towards people if the area allows for it.
10. Use variation in your voice; get louder as the speech progresses (*crescendo*).
11. Summarize at the end and thank your audience.

Advanced Tips, Not for the Faint of Heart

These storytelling tips are a bit more advanced folks, but you've made it this far, haven't you?

Movies are stories for pleasure, but storytelling in business is to incite action. Similarly, though, you still need to use structure. Here are my other tips for only the most advanced, non-dumpy leader:

1. Use your personal experiences, but customize the story to your audience every time.
2. Arouse the audience with an emotional action they can relate to.
3. There must be a struggle or opposing forces, not an argument.
4. Don't be your own hero unless you're telling your personal story.
5. The theme should be crystal clear, touching on it here and there during the story, then hammering it home at the end.

The Super Tribe and My Favorite Leader

The people in this book are my "super tribe." They make me better with the proximity of their own inspirational lives. And if you asked me who my favorite leader is from history? It's George Washington.

The story of George Washington's history is an epic tale of strategic alignment and underdog glory. He did well for a guy initially trained as a surveyor. He utilized advanced business psychology to achieve his goals, long before we had any research on the topic. Many times, his military successes were achieved despite impossible circumstances that he and only he could circumvent. I call that competitive advantage.

In product terms, victorious underdogs are disruptive innovators, like the invention and development of things such as washing machines, telephones, flash drives, Wikipedia, LED displays, hydraulics, keyboards, steamboats, the cotton gin, automobiles, private jets, Wikipedia, and those silly hover boards that light up and play music. George Washington was a disruptive leader.

He took responsibility for the leaders that would eventually take his place. He knew he had to leave behind a legacy. Build a foundation. American independence was his "glorious cause." He served as our Commander-in-Chief without pay and went home almost bankrupt. Richard Neustadt, Harvard Scholar, said, "it was the way he attended to and stuck by his men. His soldiers knew that he respected and cared for them and that he would share their severe hardships."

George valued his people and followers. George cared about others' opinions and took them to heart. (It's quite clear if you read the stories in Ron Chernow's Pulitzer Prize-winning biography of Washington.) "Associate with men of good quality if you esteem your reputation; for it is better to be alone than in bad company." From George's lips to our ears. And look who he hung out with: John Adams, Thomas Jefferson, Benjamin Franklin, Alexander Hamilton. I'm fortunate enough to have just as impressive of a posse; the remarkable leaders featured in this book. When you are near these types of people, you get feedback, motivation, support, advice, and friendship. I try to think of my leadership as a top ten list of the best skills I've picked up from others.

Back to George Washington. He lived his vision and valued his people. This is why he had such courageous underdog victories. Perseverance must have been his favorite word. He had another leadership principle: the alignment of purpose and strategy in his organization. Let's think.

What is our enduring purpose? What do we what we do? Does our vision have value? What do we offer the industry? What do customers want? How will we beat the competitors? What capabilities are required to execute our strategy (execution, agility, connectivity, innovation)? What makes us good enough to win? How good are we? What type of people, culture, structure, and process will make us good at the things we need to win at? What delivers the performance we need? What management practice systems and technologies best fit our purpose? All good questions that leaders should think about.

I Am a Robot; I Do Not Compute

Picture two coastal redwood trees, Sequoia sempervirens of the Cypress family, in Northern California. These trees have large knots because they were under extreme stress and they expressed this through the development of knots. Similar to how people get muscle knots from the excess amount of cortisol in their blood that can cause stifling muscle tension. Businesses also develop knots, and they come from lousy leadership moments that tighten up the culture like a knot. Sometimes you gotta laugh it off and turn those moments into an opportunity to practice better leadership. Don't be the knot! Be the masseuse. Prepare yourself for making a good impact on people so you can look back and be proud of what you've done. Next time you have a meeting, make it a good one. Next time you talk to your boss, leave with a smile and tell a joke. Still confused how to put this into action?

Here's a simple example. It's the holiday season, and you decide to put up a tree at the office. Do you decorate it alone after hours? No. Place the tree in a communal area with lots of foot traffic close by. Then build a station for your colleagues to write their names and cut out their do-it-yourself ornaments with a variety of fun colors, mixing in the company colors as well. Add a prize that'll be raffled off to all participants. Send a fun email announcement to the people on your floor or division about it. Get your department to kick off the excitement by being the first to make an ornament, then take them to lunch and bring some holiday jokes with you. This is a simple, enjoyable, and engaging way to decorate the tree at work.

I'm no Ferris *medical practitioner* (damn, that was bad) but research does show that humor is one of the best ways to relieve stress. It can soothe tension, reduce your stress responders, and improve your immunity, mood, and personal satisfaction. It's nature's organic painkiller that you can't overdose on! Get your daily dose of laughter by prioritizing it into your daily activities. Watch Seinfeld reruns if you have to.

Think about the things you do that a robot could replace. In the tree example above, the robot would have easily procured a tree and assembled decorations. That's not leadership. If you told the robot to design a tree-decorating experience that would improve the corporate culture, the robot would have said, "I am a robot, I do not compute." Because robots solve for efficiency, but not effectiveness, strategy, humor, and leadership. Don't be a robot.

SHIT OR GET OFF THE POT

We live in an unsettling time, but there's been a connection among all of the uncertainty. This is a complex world where leaders are failing left and right, up and down. It's tiring. But despite the distractions on social media and the overwhelming violence around the world, we must push through. Clear the noise! Are you another shadow in the crowd or a voice to be heard? Will you lead the future? It's not dichotomous, but you may be one or the other. Be the voice, we accept you.

Don't forget; the universe doesn't care about us. Death and darkness are always right around the corner. I'm not trying to be morbid, but your life is going to pass you by so you may as well make the most of it. Be inspiring and funny. Be an example for others. What do you want people to say about you when you die? Were you a skid-mark in the pants of life or the leader people needed. Will you live in the moment or will you wake up old and full of regret?

In this book, we talked about how to maximize your affective communication through storytelling, boosting your conscious mind by living in the moment and improving some of your cognitive skills that impact leadership development. I hope you will make a positive impact on the people around you. Your energy matters. Who are you going to be? Not a dingle berry!

Hopefully, you laughed a couple of times or at least smiled creepily to yourself while reading this book. In return for saving your life and mitigating your stress, all I ask is at the very least you tell a couple of jokes, for God's sake man!

Key takeaways from this book:

1. Tell personal and memorable stories.
2. Show up and be a positive energy for the world.
3. Write down your goals frequently so you can make the best use of your time.
4. Listen to people and lead by example.
5. Turn regular moments into unique opportunities to practice leadership.
6. A book about leadership/leadershit results in a lot of poop jokes.

If you shit your pants in the forest and nobody is there to smell it, did it really happen? Yes actually, it did. And, you nasty. But good things will still happen to you.

Even though it can be difficult to find examples of influential leaders in the media, politics, business, entertainment, and basically anywhere, I know you will rise above all that and be great. Thanks for reading.

We love you, New York. Goodnight!
Brian, Stephanie (and Mr. Butts)